D1623937

little book of

Vodka

Cocktails

little book of

Vodka
Cocktails

hamlyn

An Hachette Livre UK Company
First published in 2000 by Hamlyn a division of Octopus Publishing Group Limited,
2–4 Heron Quays, London E14 4JP

Copyright © 2000 Octopus Publishing Group Ltd

Distributed in the United States and Canada by Sterling Publishing Co., Inc.
387 Park Avenue South, New York, NY 10016-8810

All rights reserved. No part of this publication may be reproduced,
stored in a retrieval system, or transmitted, in any form or by any means, electronic,
electrostatic, magnetic tape, mechanical, photocopying, recording or otherwise
without the prior permission in writing of the publisher.

British Library Cataloguing-in-Publication Data
A catalogue record for this book is available from the British Library

ISBN-13: 978-0-600-61770-9
ISBN-10: 0-600-61770-X

Printed in China

10 9 8 7 6 5 4 3 2 1

Notes for American readers

The measure that has been used in the recipes is based on
a bar jigger, which is 45 ml (1½ fl oz). If preferred, a
different volume can be used providing the proportions
are kept constant within a drink and suitable adjustments
are made to spoon measurements, where they occur.

Standard level spoon measurements are used in all
recipes.
1 tablespoon = one 15 ml spoon
1 teaspoon = one 5 ml spoon
Imperial and metric measurements have been given in
some of the recipes. Use one set of measurements only
and not a mixture of both.

UK	US
caster sugar	granulated sugar
cocktail cherries	maraschino cherries
cocktail stick	toothpick
double cream	heavy cream
drinking chocolate	presweetened cocoa powder
icing sugar	confectioners' sugar
jug	pitcher
lemon rind	lemon peel or zest
single cream	light cream
soda water	club soda

Contents

CLASSICS 8

The Moscow Mule was arguably the first true
vodka cocktail and since its invention in 1941, a
complete repertoire of classics has developed from
the sophisticated Vodka Gibson to the robust Bloody
Mary and from the richly flavoured Black Russian to
the refreshing Screwdriver. All these great favourites
are included here.

PARTY COCKTAILS 38

This sparkling collection of lively cocktails will
make any party a sure-fire success, from the tried-
and-tested Vodka Martini to the up-to-the-minute
Millennium Cocktail. In fact, just serving them will
turn any occasion into a special celebration.

EXOTIC & FRUITY 66

The versatility of vodka is amply demonstrated here.
Mix it with fruit, fruit juice, liqueurs, cream, ice cream
or spices to set the taste buds tingling. Whether you
choose Frozen Steppes, Siamese Slammer or
Caribbean Cruise, you will be transported with delight.

Introduction

Just as Scotland and Ireland both claim to have invented whisky, Russia and Poland argue over the origins of vodka. The Poles reckon that they were distilling vodka as early as the eighth century, but as the spirit they produced was distilled from wine, it was probably closer to brandy. By the eleventh century, they were producing a medicinal spirit called gorzalka, which would be more or less recognizable as vodka. The first documented production of vodka in Russia dates from the end of the ninth century, although the first known distillery, at Khylnovsk, was not recorded until 1174. The word vodka, meaning 'little water', is derived from the Russian *voda* – water – but as it is called *wodka* in Poland, this is an unreliable guide to its origins. In fact, the word vodka was not officially recognized until the end of the nineteenth century, when state distilleries and standard production techniques were introduced in Russia.

Whatever its origins, the vodka of the distant past was very different from the drink produced today. It was originally distilled from potato mash – traditionally, rotting potatoes – and because of impurities and sometimes a perfectly foul taste, it was often flavoured with herbs, spices, honey, fruit, nuts and a variety of aromatics. Production techniques, including pot distillation in the fifteenth century and charcoal filtering in the eighteenth, improved over the years and vodka also began to be produced from grains, such as wheat, or molasses.

The drink that had been dubbed by the British Ambassador in the fourteenth century as 'the Russian national drink,' was first exported in 1505, to Sweden. However, it was not until the years following the Bolshevik Revolution that vodka really took off in the West. When the Communists took over the distilleries, many private vodka-makers left Russia. One of them, Smirnoff, travelled to the United States via Paris and, in 1934, the first American vodka distillery was established. Even then, interest in the spirit was limited and it was not until the swinging sixties that vodka became a popular drink among the newly independent younger generation. This coincided, perhaps not by chance, with the rediscovery of cocktails, which had gone into something of a decline following World War II.

Western vodka undergoes strict processes of distillation and filtering, which not only take out impurities, but also the natural flavour. Flavourless, colourless and odourless, it is the perfect partner for other spirits and flavourings – with the additional advantage of leaving no tell-tale signs of having been drinking on the breath. Vodka cocktails are the younger cousins of the classics based on gin, whisky or brandy that had their heyday during the 1920s, but they have become firm favourites in bars and hotels across the world. Things have now gone full circle and it has become trendy to drink flavoured vodkas once again. Some of these modern flavourings, such as chilli, seem bizarre to contemplate and it is difficult to think of many palatable cocktails based on them. However, other more traditional flavours, such as orange or peach, could provide an interesting base for a range of popular cocktail recipes.

Sugar Syrup
This may be used instead of sugar to sweeten cocktails and to give them more body. It can be bought, but is simple to make at home.

Put 4 tablespoons of caster sugar and 4 tablespoons water in a small pan and stir over a low heat until the sugar has dissolved. Bring to the boil and boil, without stirring, for 1–2 minutes. Store in a sterilized bottle in the refrigerator for up to 2 months.

Classics

Astronaut

Bloody Mary

Le Mans

Hair Raiser

Screwdriver

Godmother

Harvey Wallbanger

Vodka Collins

Vodka Gibson

Vodka Sazerac

Xantippe

Inspiration

Iceberg

Haven

Vodka Salty Dog

White Spider

Vodka Grasshopper

Moscow Mule

White Russian

Black Russian

Long Island Iced Tea

Bullshot

Astronaut

8–10 cracked ice cubes
½ measure white rum
½ measure vodka
½ measure fresh lemon
    juice
1 dash passion fruit juice
lemon wedge, to
    decorate

Put 4–5 ice cubes into a cocktail shaker and add the rum, vodka, lemon juice and passion fruit juice. Fill an old-fashioned glass with the remaining ice cubes. Shake the cocktail until a frost forms, then strain it into the glass. Decorate with the lemon wedge and serve.

Serves 1

Bloody Mary

4–5 ice cubes
juice of ½ lemon
½ teaspoon horseradish
    sauce
2 drops Worcestershire
    sauce
1 drop Tabasco sauce
2 measures thick tomato
    juice
2 measures vodka
salt and cayenne pepper

to decorate (optional)
celery stick, with the
    leaves left on
lemon or lime slice

There are many variations on this classic cocktail, invented in 1921 at Harry's Bar in Paris. Spicy or mild, naked or decorated, and the best vodka you can get hold of – although experts cannot agree which this is.

Put the ice cubes into a cocktail shaker. Pour the lemon juice, horseradish sauce, Worcestershire sauce, Tabasco sauce, tomato juice and vodka over the ice. Shake until a frost forms. Pour into a tall glass, add a pinch of salt and a pinch of cayenne and decorate with a celery stick and a lemon or lime slice, if you like.

Serves 1

Le Mans

2–3 cracked ice cubes
1 measure Cointreau
½ measure vodka
soda water
lemon slice, to decorate

Put the cracked ice into a tall glass. Add the Cointreau and vodka, stir and top up with soda water. Float the lemon slice on the top.

Serves 1

Hair Raiser

1–2 cracked ice cubes
1 measure vodka
1 measure sweet
    vermouth
1 measure tonic water
lemon and lime rind
    spirals, to decorate

Put the cracked ice into a tall
glass and pour over the vodka,
vermouth and tonic. Stir lightly.
Decorate with the lemon and
lime rind spirals and serve
with a straw.

Serves 1

Tip

To make cracked ice, put
some ice cubes into a
strong polythene bag
and hit the bag with a
rolling pin.

Screwdriver

2–3 ice cubes
1½ measures vodka
freshly squeezed orange
   juice

Put the ice cubes into a tumbler.
Add the vodka, top up with
orange juice and stir lightly.

Serves 1

Variation

Substitute apple juice for
the orange juice.
Decorate with a mint sprig.

Godmother

2–3 cracked ice cubes
1½ measures vodka
½ measure Amaretto di
    Saronno

Put the ice cubes into a tumbler.
Add the vodka and Amaretto. Stir
lightly and serve.

Serves 1

Variation

To make a Godchild,
shake 1 measure each of
vodka, Amaretto and
double cream with ice.
Strain into a cocktail
glass and serve.

Harvey Wallbanger

6 ice cubes
1 measure vodka
3 measures fresh
    orange juice
1–2 teaspoons Galliano
orange slices, to
    decorate

This is a cocktail from the 1960s, named after a Californian surfer called Harvey who drank so many Screwdrivers topped with Galliano that, as he tried to find his way out of the bar, he banged and bounced from one wall to the other.

Put half the ice cubes into a cocktail shaker and the remainder into a tall glass. Add the vodka and orange juice to the cocktail shaker. Shake well for about 30 seconds, then strain into the glass. Float the Galliano on top. Decorate with orange slices and serve with straws.

Serves 1

Vodka Collins

6 ice cubes
2 measures vodka
juice of 1 lime
1 teaspoon caster sugar
soda water

to decorate
lemon or lime slice
maraschino cherry

Put half the ice cubes into a cocktail shaker and add the vodka, lime juice and sugar and shake until a frost forms. Strain into a large tumbler, add the remaining ice and top up with soda water. Decorate with lemon or lime slices and a cherry.

Serves 1

Vodka Gibson

6 ice cubes
1 measure vodka
½ measure dry vermouth
pearl onion

Put the ice cubes into a cocktail shaker and add the vodka and vermouth. Shake until a frost forms, then strain into a cocktail glass and decorate with the pearl onion.

Serves 1

Vodka Sazerac

1 sugar cube
2 drops Angostura bitters
3 drops Pernod
2–3 ice cubes
2 measures vodka
lemonade

Put the sugar cube into an old-fashioned glass and shake the bitters on to it. Add the Pernod and swirl it about so that it clings to the side of the glass. Drop in the ice cubes and pour in the vodka. Top up with lemonade, then stir gently.

Serves 1

Xantippe

4–5 ice cubes
1 measure cherry brandy
1 measure yellow
    Chartreuse
2 measures vodka

Put the ice cubes into a mixing glass. Pour the cherry brandy, Chartreuse and vodka over the ice and stir vigorously. Strain into a chilled cocktail glass.

Serves 1

Tip

Yellow Chartreuse is a herb-based liqueur made by French monks. It has a lower alcoholic content than the green variety.

Inspiration

4–5 ice cubes
½ measure Bénédictine
½ measure dry vermouth
2 measures vodka
lime rind spiral, to
    decorate

Put the ice cubes into a mixing glass. Pour the Bénédictine, vermouth and vodka over the ice. Stir vigorously, then strain into a chilled cocktail glass and decorate with the lime spiral.

Serves 1

Iceberg

4–6 ice cubes
1½ measures vodka
1 dash Pernod

Put the ice cubes into an old-fashioned glass. Pour in the vodka and add a dash of Pernod.

Serves 1

Haven

2–3 ice cubes
1 tablespoon grenadine
1 measure Pernod
1 measure vodka
soda water

Put the ice cubes into an old-fashioned glass. Dash the grenadine over the ice, then pour in the Pernod and vodka. Top up with soda water.

Serves 1

Vodka Salty Dog

salt
6–8 ice cubes
1 measure vodka
4 measures grapefruit
    juice

Salt the rim of a large goblet and fill with ice. Add the vodka and grapefruit juice and stir.

Serves 1

White Spider

2 measures vodka
1 measure clear crème
    de menthe
crushed ice (optional)

Pour the vodka and crème de
menthe into a cocktail shaker.
Shake and pour into a chilled
cocktail glass or over crushed ice.

Serves 1

Vodka Grasshopper

1½ measures vodka
1½ measures green
    crème de menthe
1½ measures crème de
    cacao
crushed ice

Pour the vodka, crème de menthe
and crème de cacao into a
cocktail shaker half-filled with ice.
Shake and strain into a chilled
cocktail glass.

Serves 1

Moscow Mule

3–4 cracked ice cubes
2 measures vodka
juice of 2 limes
ginger beer
lime or orange slices,
    to decorate

This cocktail is one of those happy accidents. It was invented in 1941 by an employee of a US drinks firm in conjunction with a Los Angeles bar owner who was overstocked with ginger beer.

Put the cracked ice into a cocktail shaker. Add the vodka and lime juice and shake until a frost forms. Pour into a tall glass, top up with ginger beer and stir gently. Decorate with lime or orange slices.

Serves 1

White Russian

classics

6 cracked ice cubes
1 measure vodka
1 measure Tía María
1 measure milk or double
  cream

Put half the ice cubes into a cocktail shaker and add the vodka, Tía María and milk or double cream. Shake until a frost forms. Put the remaining ice cubes into a tall narrow glass and strain the cocktail over them. Serve with a straw.

Serves 1

Black Russian

4–6 cracked ice cubes
2 measures vodka
1 measure Kahlúa coffee
  liqueur
chocolate stick, to
  decorate (optional)

Put the cracked ice into a short glass. Add the vodka and Kahlúa and stir. Decorate with a chocolate stick, if you like.

Serves 1

Long Island Iced Tea

6 cracked ice cubes
½ measure vodka
½ measure gin
½ measure white rum
½ measure tequila
½ measure Cointreau
1 measure lemon juice
½ teaspoon sugar syrup
(see page 7)
cola, to top up
lemon wedge, to
decorate

Put half the ice cubes into a mixing glass. Add the vodka, gin, rum, tequila, Cointreau, lemon juice and sugar syrup. Stir well, then strain into a tall glass almost filled with ice. Top up with cola and decorate with the wedge of lemon. Serve with a straw.

Serves 1

Bullshot

6 ice cubes (optional)
1½ measures vodka
4 measures beef
    consommé (hot or
    chilled)
dash of Worcestershire
    sauce
salt and pepper

Put the ice cubes, if using, into a cocktail shaker and add the vodka, consommé and Worcestershire sauce and season lightly with salt and pepper. Shake well. Strain into a large glass or a handled glass, if serving hot.

Serves 1

Variation

This is said to be a good hangover cure. As a variation, try 1 measure vodka, 1 measure tomato juice and 1 measure beef consommé. Mix the ingredients in a tall glass half-filled with ice. Add a squeeze of lemon.

Party Cocktails

Vodka Martini

Vodka Sour

Blue Champagne

Head-over-Heels

Millennium Cocktail

Bellini-tini

Road Runner

One of Those

Sea Breeze

Cosmopolitan

Madras

Machete

Vodka Twister Fizz

Down-under Fizz

Vodka Limeade

Vodka, Lime & Soda

Snapdragon

Polish Honey Drink

Warsaw Cocktail

Vodka Martini

4–5 cracked ice cubes
¼ measure dry vermouth
3 measures vodka
green olive or a twist of
    lemon rind, to decorate

**In some circles this
concoction is known as
a Kangaroo.**

Put the ice cubes into a mixing
glass. Pour the vermouth and
vodka over the ice and stir
vigorously. Strain into a chilled
cocktail glass, drop in the olive
or decorate with a twist of
lemon rind.

Serves 1

Vodka Sour

4–5 ice cubes

2 measures vodka

½ measure sugar syrup
(see page 7)

1 egg white

1½ measures fresh
lemon juice

3 drops Angostura
bitters, to decorate

Put the ice cubes into a cocktail shaker, add the vodka, sugar syrup, egg white and lemon juice and shake until a frost forms. Pour without straining into a cocktail glass and shake 3 drops of Angostura bitters on the top to decorate.

Serves 1

Blue Champagne

4–6 ice cubes

1 measure vodka

2 tablespoons fresh
    lemon juice

2–3 dashes triple sec

2–3 dashes blue curaçao

chilled Champagne, to
    top up

Put the ice cubes into a cocktail
shaker, add the vodka, lemon
juice, triple sec and blue curaçao
and shake well. Strain into a
Champagne flute and top up
with Champagne.

Serves 1

Variation

Another vodka and
Champagne combination
is the Bucked-up Fizz.
Pour 2 measures of
orange juice and
½ measure of vodka into
a Champagne flute. Top
up with Champagne.

Head-over-Heels

4–5 ice cubes
juice of 1 lime or lemon
1 teaspoon sugar syrup
(see page 7)
3 measures vodka
3 drops Angostura bitters
Champagne, to top up
strawberry, to decorate

Put the ice cubes into a cocktail shaker. Pour the lime or lemon juice, sugar syrup, vodka and bitters over the ice and shake until a frost forms. Pour without straining into a highball glass, top up with Champagne and decorate with a strawberry.

Serves 1

Millennium Cocktail

4–5 cracked ice cubes
1 measure vodka
1 measure fresh
   raspberry juice
1 measure fresh orange
   juice
4 measures Champagne
   or sparkling dry white
   wine, chilled

Put the ice cubes into a cocktail shaker, add the vodka, raspberry juice and orange juice and shake until a frost forms. Strain into a Champagne glass and pour in the Champagne.

Serves 1

Bellini-tini

4–5 cracked ice cubes
2 measures vodka
½ measure peach
  schnapps
1 teaspoon peach juice
Champagne, to top up
peach slices, to decorate

Put the ice cubes into a cocktail shaker and add the vodka, peach schnapps and peach juice. Shake until a frost forms. Strain into a chilled cocktail glass and top up with Champagne. Decorate with peach slices.

Serves 1

Road Runner

6 cracked ice cubes
2 measures vodka
1 measure Amaretto di
    Saronno
1 measure coconut milk
grated nutmeg, to
    decorate

Put the cracked ice into a cocktail shaker and add the vodka, Amaretto and coconut milk. Shake until a frost forms, then strain into a cocktail glass. Sprinkle with a pinch of grated nutmeg.

Serves 1

One of Those

4–6 ice cubes

1 measure vodka

4 measures cranberry
juice

2 dashes Amaretto di
Saronno

juice of ½ lime

lime slice, to decorate

Half-fill a highball glass with ice cubes. Pour the vodka, cranberry juice, Amaretto and lime juice into a cocktail shaker. Shake thoroughly, pour into the highball glass and decorate with a lime slice.

Serves 1

Variation

This tasty cocktail was created in London by one inventive Australian and two thirsty Americans.

Sea Breeze

5 crushed ice cubes
1 measure vodka
1½ measures cranberry
    juice
1½ measures fresh
    grapefruit juice
lime slice, to decorate

**This is one of those drinks
that has changed
considerably over the
years. In the 1930s it was
made with gin rather than
vodka and with grenadine
and lemon juice instead of
cranberry juice and
grapefruit juice.**

Put the crushed ice into a tall
glass, pour over the vodka,
cranberry juice and grapefruit
juice and stir well. Decorate with
a lime slice and serve with
a straw.

Serves 1

Variation

To make a Cape
Cod(der), mix 1 measure
of vodka, 2 measures of
cranberry juice and add a
dash of lemon juice.

Cosmopolitan

6 cracked ice cubes
1 measure vodka
½ measure Cointreau
1 measure cranberry
    juice
juice of ½ lime
lime slice, to decorate

Put the cracked ice into a cocktail shaker and add the vodka, Cointreau, cranberry juice and lime juice. Shake until a frost forms. Strain into a cocktail glass and decorate with a lime slice.

Serves 1

Madras

6–8 ice cubes
1 measure vodka
1 measure orange juice
2 measures cranberry
    juice
orange or lime slice, to
    decorate

Half-fill a tall glass with ice. Pour over the vodka, orange juice and cranberry juice and decorate with a fruit slice.

Serves 1

Machete

4–6 ice cubes
1 measure vodka
2 measures pineapple
    juice
3 measures tonic water

Fill a tall glass or wine glass with ice cubes. Pour the vodka, pineapple juice and tonic into a mixing glass. Stir, then pour into the glass.

Serves 1

Vodka Twister Fizz

4–5 ice cubes
juice of 1 lemon
½ teaspoon sugar syrup
(see page 7)
1 egg white
3 drops Pernod
3 measures vodka
ginger ale
lime slice, to decorate

Put the ice cubes into a cocktail shaker. Pour the lemon juice, sugar syrup, egg white, Pernod and vodka over the ice and shake until a frost forms. Pour without straining into a highball glass and top up with ginger ale. Stir once or twice and decorate with a lime slice.

Serves 1

Down-under Fizz

4–5 ice cubes
juice of 1 lemon
juice of ½ orange
½ teaspoon grenadine
3 measures vodka
soda water

Put the ice cubes into a cocktail shaker. Pour the lemon juice, orange juice, grenadine and vodka over the ice and shake until a frost forms. Pour without straining into a highball glass and top up with soda water. Serve with a straw.

Serves 1

Vodka Limeade

6 limes
125 g (4 oz) caster sugar
750 ml (1¼ pints) boiling
    water
salt
8 measures vodka
ice cubes
lime wedges, to decorate

Halve the limes, then squeeze the juice into a large jug. Put the squeezed halves into a heatproof bowl with the sugar and boiling water and leave to infuse for 15 minutes. Add a pinch of salt, give the infusion a good stir then strain it into the jug with the lime juice and add the vodka. Add 6 ice cubes, cover and refrigerate for 2 hours, or until chilled. To serve, place 3–4 ice cubes in each glass and pour the limeade over them. Decorate each glass with a lime wedge.

Serves 8

Tip

If you roll the whole limes around quite hard on a board with your hand, you will find that you get more juice from them.

Vodka, Lime & Soda

6–8 ice cubes
1 measure vodka
2 measures lime cordial
    or lime juice
soda water
lime slice, to decorate

Half-fill a tall glass with ice cubes. Pour in the vodka and lime cordial or lime juice, top up with soda water and stir. Decorate with a lime slice.

Serves 1

Variation

A quick fix of this combination is called a Cosmos. Pour 1 measure vodka and ½ measure freshly squeezed lime juice into a cocktail shaker half-filled with ice. Shake well and strain into a shot glass.

Snapdragon

4–6 ice cubes

2 measures vodka

4 measures green crème
    de menthe

soda water

mint sprigs, to decorate

Fill a highball glass with ice cubes. Add the vodka and crème de menthe and stir. Top up with soda water. Decorate with a mint sprig.

Serves 1

Polish Honey Drink

6 tablespoons clear
  honey
300 ml (½ pint) water
4 cloves
7.5 cm (3 inch) piece of
  cinnamon stick
1 vanilla pod
2 long lemon rind strips
2 long orange rind strips
1 bottle vodka
  (750 ml/1¼ pints)

Put the honey and water into a saucepan and heat gently until the honey has dissolved. Add the cloves, cinnamon stick, vanilla pod, lemon rind and orange rind. Bring to the boil and simmer for 5 minutes. Cover the pan, remove from the heat and leave to infuse for 1 hour. Strain and return to the rinsed pan. Add the vodka and bring to just below simmering point over a low heat and warm through for 5 minutes. Serve in warmed handled glasses or mugs.

Serves 8

Warsaw Cocktail

6 ice cubes
1 measure vodka
½ measure blackberry-
   flavoured brandy
½ measure dry vermouth
1 teaspoon fresh lemon
   juice

Put the ice cubes into a cocktail shaker and add the vodka, brandy, vermouth and lemon juice. Shake until a frost forms. Strain into a cocktail glass and serve.

Serves 1

Exotic & Fruity

Siamese Slammer

Cool Wind

Chi Chi

Blue Moon

Sloe Comfortable Screw

Cranberry Crush

Vodka & Watermelon Crush

Frozen Steppes

Creamsickle

Vodka Daiquiri

Cherry Vodka Julep

Melon Ball

Caribbean Cruise

Monkey's Delight

Sex on the Beach

Hairy Fuzzy Navel

Vodka Caipirinha

Mudslide

Russian Coffee

Hawaiian Vodka

Lemon Drop

Kamikaze

Siamese Slammer

3 measures vodka
juice of 2 oranges
1 small ripe papaya,
    peeled and chopped
1 banana, sliced
juice of 1 lime
3 measures sugar syrup
    (see page 7)
8 crushed ice cubes
4 papaya slices, to
    decorate

Put all the ingredients into a blender and process until smooth. Serve in tall glasses, each decorated with a slice of papaya.

Serves 4

Cool Wind

4–5 ice cubes
1 measure dry vermouth
juice of ½ grapefruit
½ teaspoon Cointreau
3 measures vodka

Put the ice cubes into a mixing glass. Pour the vermouth, grapefruit juice, Cointreau and vodka over the ice. Stir gently, then strain into a chilled cocktail glass.

Serves 1

Chi Chi

2 measures vodka
1 measure coconut
    cream
4 measures pineapple
    juice
6 crushed ice cubes

to decorate
pineapple slice
maraschino cherry

Put the vodka, coconut cream, pineapple juice and crushed ice into a blender and process until smooth. Pour into a tall glass and decorate with a slice of pineapple and a cherry.

Serves 1

Blue Moon

5 cracked ice cubes
¾ measure vodka
¾ measure tequila
1 measure blue curaçao
lemonade

Put half the ice into a mixing glass and add the vodka, tequila and blue curaçao. Stir to mix. Put the remaining ice into a tall glass and strain in the cocktail. Top up with lemonade and serve with a straw.

Serves 1

Sloe Comfortable Screw

6–8 ice cubes
½ measure sloe gin
½ measure Southern
    Comfort
1 measure vodka
2½ measures orange
    juice

The name of this drink is an easy way of remembering what goes into it. Sloe for the sloe gin, Comfortable for the Southern Comfort and Screw, short for Screwdriver – vodka and orange juice.

Variation

To make a Sloe Comfortable Screw Up Against the Wall, mix the drink as above and top with Galliano. The final part of the name derives from the place where the tall, slender bottle of Galliano is usually kept in a bar.

Half-fill a tall glass with ice cubes. Pour the sloe gin, Southern Comfort, vodka and orange juice into the glass and stir well.

Serves 1

Cranberry Crush

600 ml (1 pint) cranberry
    juice
600 ml (1 pint) fresh
    orange juice
150 ml (¼ pint) water
½ teaspoon ground
    ginger
½ teaspoon mixed spice
sugar
1 bottle vodka
    (750 ml/1¼ pints)

to decorate
kumquats
cranberries
mint sprigs

Place the cranberry juice, orange juice, water, ginger and mixed spice in a saucepan and bring to the boil over a low heat. Stir in sugar to taste, then simmer for 5 minutes. Remove from the heat and stir in the vodka. Pour into punch cups, decorate with kumquats, cranberries and mint sprigs. Alternatively, serve chilled for a summer party.

Serves 10

Vodka & Watermelon Crush

1 large or 2 small ripe
    watermelons, chilled
300 ml (½ pint) fresh
    orange juice
juice of 1 lime
3 measures vodka
sugar
crushed ice
watermelon slices,
    to decorate

Cut the watermelon into quarters and remove the skin and seeds. Roughly chop the flesh and put it into a blender or food processor with the orange juice, lime juice and vodka. Add sugar to taste and process until smooth. Fill 2–3 glasses with crushed ice and pour in the drink. Add a watermelon slice to each glass to decorate.

Serves 2–3

Frozen Steppes

1 measure vodka
1 measure dark crème
    de cacao
1 scoop vanilla ice cream
maraschino cherry, to
    decorate

Put the vodka, crème de cacao
and ice cream into a blender and
process for a few seconds. Pour
into a large wine glass and
decorate with a cherry.

Serves 1

Creamsickle

6 cracked ice cubes
1 measure vodka
1 measure triple sec
1 measure white crème
    de cacao
1 measure single cream

Put the cracked ice into a cocktail shaker and add the vodka, triple sec, crème de cacao and cream. Shake until a frost forms, then pour into a highball glass.

Serves 1

Vodka Daiquiri

exotic & fruity

6 cracked ice cubes
1 measure vodka
1 teaspoon sugar
juice of ½ lime or lemon

Put the cracked ice into a cocktail shaker and add the vodka, sugar and lime or lemon juice. Shake until a frost forms. Strain into a cocktail glass.

Serves 1

Variation

To make a frozen daiquiri, combine the vodka, sugar and lime or lemon juice in a blender with a handful of crushed ice. Process for a few seconds on low speed, then at high speed until firm. Decorate with a slice of lime and a cherry and serve with a straw.

Cherry Vodka Julep

8 cracked ice cubes

juice of ½ lemon

1 teaspoon sugar or
   sugar syrup (see
   page 7)

1 teaspoon grenadine

1 measure cherry brandy

3 measures vodka

1 measure sloe gin

to decorate

1 lemon slice

1 orange slice

Fill a tall glass with cracked ice.
Put 3–4 ice cubes into a mixing
glass and pour in the lemon
juice, sugar or sugar syrup,
grenadine, cherry brandy, vodka
and sloe gin. Stir, then strain into
the ice-filled glass. Decorate with
the lemon and orange slices.

Serves 1

exotic & fruity

Melon Ball

5 cracked ice cubes
1 measure vodka
1 measure Midori
1 measure orange juice,
    plus extra for
    topping up

to decorate
orange slice
small ball of banana

Put the cracked ice into a tall glass or goblet. Pour the vodka, Midori and orange juice into a cocktail shaker. Shake well to mix, then strain into the glass. Top up with more orange juice if necessary. Decorate with the fruit and serve with a straw.

Serves 1

Caribbean Cruise

10–12 ice cubes
1 measure vodka
¼ measure light rum
¼ measure coconut rum
1 dash of grenadine
2 measures pineapple
    juice
pineapple slice, to
    decorate

Put 6 ice cubes into a cocktail shaker and add the vodka, both kinds of rum and a dash of grenadine. Shake until a frost forms. Half-fill a tall glass with ice cubes, strain the cocktail over the ice and add the pineapple juice. Decorate with a pineapple slice.

Serves 1

Monkey's Delight

1 measure vodka
½ measure crème de banane
½ measure dark crème de cacao
1 banana
2 scoops vanilla ice cream
½ measure single cream

Put the vodka, crème de banane, crème de cacao, ¾ of the banana, the ice cream and cream in a blender and process until smooth. Pour into a tall glass. Decorate with the reserved banana, cut into slices.

Serves 1

Sex on the Beach

3 ice cubes
½ measure vodka
½ measure peach
    schnapps
1 measure cranberry
    juice
1 measure orange juice
1 measure pineapple
    juice (optional)
maraschino cherry, to
    decorate

Put the ice into a cocktail shaker and add the vodka, peach schnapps, cranberry juice, orange juice and pineapple juice, if using. Shake until a frost forms. Pour into a tall glass, decorate with the cherry and serve with a straw.

Serves 1

Hairy Fuzzy Navel

6 cracked ice cubes
1 measure peach schnapps
1½ measures vodka
1 tablespoon orange juice

Put the cracked ice into a cocktail shaker and add the peach schnapps, vodka and orange juice. Shake until a frost forms, then strain into a cocktail glass.

Serves 1

Variation

A Fuzzy Navel is made without the vodka.

Vodka Caipirinha

6 lime wedges
2 teaspoons brown sugar
2 measures vodka
crushed ice

This is a vodka variation of the authentic cocktail which is traditionally made with cachaça, a Brazilian spirit made from rum and sugar cane.

Place 3 of the lime wedges in a large tumbler or old-fashioned glass and add the brown sugar and vodka. Mix well, mashing the lime wedges slightly to release a little juice. Top up with crushed ice and decorate with the remaining lime wedges.

Serves 1

Mudslide

exotic & fruity

10 cracked ice cubes
1 measure vodka
1 measure Kahlúa
1 measure Baileys Irish
    Cream

Put 6 cracked ice cubes into a cocktail shaker and add the vodka, Kahlúa and Baileys. Shake until a frost forms. Strain into a tumbler and add the remaining cracked ice.

Serves 1

Russian Coffee

½ measure vodka
½ measure coffee liqueur
½ measure double cream
crushed ice

Put the vodka, coffee liqueur, cream and crushed ice into a blender and process for about 15 seconds. Strain into a cocktail glass and serve.

Serves 1

Tip

Before taking a sip of this drink, why not toast to your health with the customary Russian and Polish toast *na zdrowie*?

Hawaiian Vodka

4–5 ice cubes
1 measure pineapple
    juice
juice of 1 lemon
juice of 1 orange
1 teaspoon grenadine
3 measures vodka
lemon slice, to decorate

Put the ice cubes into a cocktail shaker. Add the pineapple juice, lemon juice, orange juice, grenadine and vodka and shake until a frost forms. Strain into a tumbler, decorate with a lemon slice and serve with a straw.

Serves 1

Lemon Drop

6 cracked ice cubes
1 measure vodka
lemon wedge
sugar, for dipping

Put the cracked ice into a cocktail shaker and add the vodka. Strain into a shot glass. Dip the lemon wedge in the sugar. Drink the vodka, then suck on the lemon immediately.

Serves 1

Kamikaze

6 cracked ice cubes
½ measure vodka
½ measure triple sec
½ measure lime juice

Put the cracked ice into a cocktail shaker and add the vodka, triple sec and lime juice. Shake until a frost forms, then strain into a shot glass.

Serves 1

INDEX

Acknowledgements

Octopus Publishing Group
Ltd./Jean Cazals 45
  /Sandra Lane 95
  /Neil Mersh 19, 23, 41, 46, 49,
  58, 59, 83, 89, 93
  /Peter Myers 38, 55, 71
  /William Reavell Cover, 2, 3, 5,
  6-7, 8, 11, 13, 16, 21, 25,
  27, 29, 30, 33, 34, 43, 51,
  53, 57, 61, 64, 66, 68, 72,
  75, 77, 80, 84

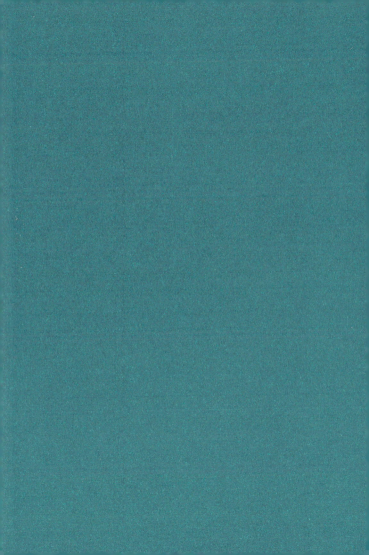